For permission to include copyright material,
acknowledgment and thanks are due to the following:

Methuen Children's Books Ltd for *Hedgehog's Magic* from
"Hedgehog and Puppy Dog Tales" by Ruth Manning-Sanders;
The Tiger Who Liked Baths from "Upside Down Stories" by
Donald Bisset and *Step on a Crack* from "Time for One More"
by Leila Berg.

Harrap Ltd for *The Little Wooden Horse* from
"The Adventures of the Little Wooden Horse" by Ursula Moray Williams;
Milly-Molly-Mandy has a Surprise from "More of Milly-Molly-Mandy"
by Joyce Lankester Brisley and *Teddy Robinson's Night Out*
from "Teddy Robinson's Omnibus" by Joan G. Robinson

The Bodley Head for *The Stamping Elephant* by Anita Hewett
from "The Anita Hewett Animal Story Book"

Century Hutchinson Publishing Group Ltd for *Mr. Puffblow's Hat*
and *The Potato with Big Ideas* from "Little Old Mrs Pepperpot"
by Alf Prøysen

Dr. Frank L. Gilbert for *The Little Girl Who Got Out of Bed
the Wrong Side* by Ruth Ainsworth.

Faber and Faber Ltd for *Tim Rabbit's Sneeze* from
"The Adventures of Tim Rabbit" by Alison Uttley

Town Mouse, Country Mouse is retold by
Linda Yeatman and in this version is © Grisewood and Dempsey Ltd

This edition published in 1993 by Mimosa Books,
distributed by Outlet Book Company, Inc., a Random
House Company, 40 Engelhard Avenue, Avenel,
New Jersey 07001.

2 4 6 8 10 9 7 5 3 1

First published in 1989 by Grisewood & Dempsey Ltd.
Copyright © Grisewood & Dempsey Ltd. 1989

ISBN 1 85698 506 7

Printed and bound in Italy

STORIES AND RHYMES FOR UNDER FIVES

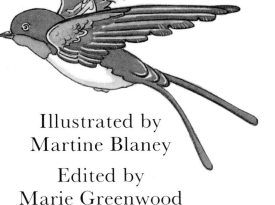

Illustrated by
Martine Blaney

Edited by
Marie Greenwood

MIMOSA
·BOOKS·

NEW YORK · AVENEL, NEW JERSEY

Contents

Thumbelina

Hans Christian Andersen

There was once a woman who wanted a child very much indeed. She went to visit a good fairy and asked her for her help. The fairy gave her a very special grain of barley which the woman took home and planted in a flowerpot. The grain grew into a beautiful pink flower. One day, the woman bent over and kissed its closed petals. Immediately they opened up to show a tiny girl—no bigger than the woman's thumb. "I will call her 'Thumbelina'", she said happily.

Thumbelina slept in a bed made from a walnut shell and she used flower petals as a bed cover. During the day Thumbelina liked to play in the kitchen sink, using a thimble as a boat to sail in.

One evening when Thumbelina was sleeping softly in her walnut-bed an ugly toad hopped in through an open window. He saw the little girl and thought how pretty she was. He took hold of the walnut shell and carried it away with him with the pretty little Thumbelina still sleeping inside.

He came to some lilies on a big river, and put Thumbelina down on a lily leaf. The tiny girl woke up and cried out in dismay to find she was not safe at home. The Toad said to her, "You are to be my wife. I shall go and prepare our home deep down in the mud." With that he disappeared under the water.

Poor Thumbelina started to cry. She did not want to marry the big ugly Toad. The little fishes that swam in the river heard her crying and felt sorry for her. "We must help her," they said. They swam around the stem that held the lily leaf to the riverbed and started to bite through it. At last the lily broke free and drifted down the river. "Farewell, pretty one, farewell," the fishes cried.

The lily leaf carried Thumbelina a long way. Finally, the leaf was caught in some rushes at the side of the river. Thumbelina managed to climb out on to dry land. It started to snow and Thumbelina wrapped herself up in a leaf to keep warm.

The days went by and still it snowed. Poor Thumbelina felt cold and miserable. "Oh if only someone could help me!" she cried.

By chance, she came upon a fieldmouse who was about to go into his home. "Can you help me Mr. Mouse?" she asked. "I have no food and nowhere to keep warm." Now the Fieldmouse was a very kind little mouse and he asked Thumbelina to come and stay with him in his warm home.

Thumbelina was very happy with the Fieldmouse. But one day the

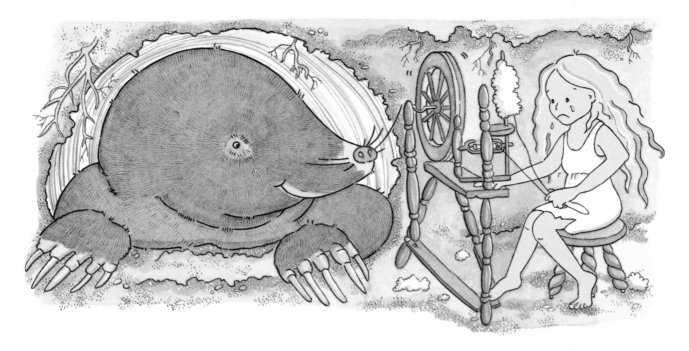

Mole, the Fieldmouse's neighbor, came to visit. The Mole was very grand in his black fur coat, and he asked Thumbelina to marry him.

The Fieldmouse was so happy he answered for Thumbelina before she had a chance to say anything! "Thumbelina would be honored to marry you," he said. The gentle Thumbelina did not know what to do: she did not want to hurt the Fieldmouse's feelings by disagreeing with him, but neither did she want to marry the Mole and live deep down underground, so she stayed silent.

It was arranged that they should marry in one year's time. Thumbelina went to visit the Mole every day and she would walk through a dark tunnel to get to his home. One day, she noticed a tiny bird lying at the side of the tunnel. She bent down and saw that the poor thing was hardly breathing. She went to gather some leaves and with them she made a bed for the bird. From that day on she stopped and nursed the little bird on her way to see the Mole. After a while the bird was fit enough to fly. "Thank you, kind Thumbelina, for saving my life!" he called, and flew out of the tunnel into the sunlight.

The wedding day drew closer. Now when Thumbelina visited the Mole she would sit and spin white thread for her wedding dress. The Mole would sit and silently watch her.

Finally the wedding day dawned. Thumbelina was very sad. She stepped out to look at the sunlight for the last time. Suddenly, the bird that she had saved flew over her. "Come away with me!" he cried. The bird swooped down and Thumbelina climbed on to his back and he flew off with her in an instant.

The little bird flew and flew until they came to a beautiful place where the birds sang and the sun shone and flowers grew everywhere. In each of the flowers there lived a tiny person as little as Thumbelina. The bird placed Thumbelina in one very beautiful white flower and then flew away calling goodbye to the sweet Thumbelina.

Now, inside this flower lived the King of the Flower People. He fell in love at once with Thumbelina and asked her to marry him. "I would be very happy to, dear King," said Thumbelina softly. And so they were married and lived happily ever after in the Kingdom of Flowers.

Mary's Lamb

Mary had a little lamb,
Its fleece was white as snow;
And everywhere that Mary went
The lamb was sure to go.

It had followed her to school one day,
That was against the rule;
It made the children laugh and play
To see a lamb at school.

And so the teacher turned it out,
But still it lingered near,
And waited patiently about
Till Mary did appear.

Why does the lamb love Mary so?
The eager children cry;
Why, Mary loves the lamb, you know,
The teacher did reply.

Hedgehog's Magic

Ruth Manning-Sanders

One morning Hedgehog was trotting through the forest when she met Tiger.

Tiger was out looking for his breakfast. When he saw Hedgehog he said, "Ha! The very thing! I am so hungry, Hedgehog, I am going to eat you!"

Hedgehog was terribly frightened, but she spoke up bravely. "Eat *me!* You wouldn't dare! I may be small, but I am far more dangerous than you are!"

"*You* dangerous?" said Tiger.

"Yes," said Hedgehog. "All the creatures are afraid of me, because you see I have magic powers."

"Rubbish!" said Tiger.

"It's true," said Hedgehog. "I can prove it to you. I'll just walk down this path through the forest and you will see how frightened the creatures will be. They will all rush away when they see me. And you

can come close behind me so that I can't escape you.''

Tiger was so astonished to hear that all the creatures were afraid of Hedgehog that he forgot how hungry he was. "Oh very well, show me,'' he said.

So they set off along the path through the forest, Hedgehog in front and Tiger following close behind.

By and by they met a big deer with long sharp horns. Deer was nibbling leaves from a tree; but directly he saw Hedgehog and Tiger coming he wheeled around and fled for his life.

"There you are!'' said Hedgehog. "What did I tell you?''

"Well I never would have believed it!'' said Tiger. "But after all it was only a deer. All deer are cowards.''

"Ah, but you wait!'' said Hedgehog.

So they walked on farther, Hedgehog ahead and Tiger keeping close behind her.

Rounding a corner, they came upon a big black bear. Bear was so busy picking berries from a bush that at first he didn't see Hedgehog and Tiger. But Hedgehog gave a loud "*Ahem!*" Bear looked around. He saw Hedgehog and Tiger. He gave an angry growl and lumbered off as fast as he could go.

Tiger was amazed. "Why on earth should a great big chap like Bear be afraid of a little shrimp like you?"

"Aha!" said Hedgehog. "That's my secret. I have never told anybody yet, and I never will tell anybody!"

So they went on together around another corner, and there was the great wild boar, the grouchiest creature in the forest. As soon as Boar saw them, his eyes flashed red with rage and he bristled for the attack. But all at once he changed his mind and bounded away as if shot from a cannon.

Tiger could hardly believe his eyes. He began to feel nervous.

Just then they came to a high road that crossed through the forest. Riding down the road was a party of young men on horseback.

"Now you watch," said Hedgehog. "I'll stand in the middle of the road. Those young fellows won't dare to pass *me!*"

Hedgehog and Tiger stood in the middle of the road. And to Tiger's utter astonishment, as soon as the young men caught sight of them, they swung their horses around and galloped back the way they had come.

Tiger was now really frightened of Hedgehog.

The Owl and the Pussy-Cat

Edward Lear

The Owl and the Pussy-Cat went to sea
   In a beautiful pea-green boat:
They took some honey, and plenty of money
   Wrapped up in a five-pound note.
The Owl looked up to the stars above,
   And sand to a small guitar,
"O lovely Pussy, O Pussy, my love,
What a beautiful Pussy you are,
          You are,
          You are!
What a beautiful Pussy you are!"

Pussy said to the Owl, "You elegant fowl,
    How charmingly sweet you sing!
Oh! Let us be married; too long we have tarried:
    But what shall we do for a ring?"
They sailed away, for a year and a day,
    To the land, where the bong-tree grows;
And there in a wood a Piggy-wig stood,
    With a ring at the end of his nose,
                His nose,
                His nose,
With a ring at the end of his nose.

"Dear Pig, are you willing to sell for one shilling
    You ring?" Said the Piggy, "I will."
So they took it away, and were married next day
    By the turkey who lives on the hill.
They dined on mince and slices of quince,
    Which they ate with a runcible spoon;
And hand in hand, on the edge of the sand,
    They danced by the light of the moon,
                The moon,
                The moon,
They danced by the light of the moon.

Step on a Crack

Leila Berg

Once there was a bear, who was very careful not to step on the cracks. "If you step on a crack," said his mother, "you'll turn into a child." So the little bear walked very carefully in the streets.

But one day he tried too hard not to step on the cracks.

He wobbled.

He almost fell.

He stepped on a crack.

And just as his mother had said, he turned into a child.

He had no idea how to behave. He had always been a bear before. So he growled. "Come away from that child," said the mothers to the other children. "He's wild."

He snuffled. "Come away from that child," said the mothers to the other children. "He's infectious."

He walked on four feet. "Come away from that child," said the mothers to the other children. "He's peculiar."

He climbed up a lamp-post. "Come away from that child," said the mothers to the other children. "He's gone too far."

Some of the mothers sent for a doctor. Some for a policeman. The little bear didn't like either. He stayed at the top of the lamp-post.

It grew darker. Darker still. Now it was time for the lamp to go on. How would the bear manage to hold on when his paw got hot with the lamp, and the lamp shone into his eyes?

But just at that very moment, another mother and another child came around the corner. They knew nothing of what had been happening and the mother was saying to the child, "Step carefully. If you step on a crack, you'll turn into a bear."

"*Into a bear!*" The little bear slid down the lamp-post just as the light went on. The doctor and the policeman were waiting for him, but he put his foot firmly and positively and quite unmistakably on a crack. "*There!*" he said.

And he turned back into a bear.

Three Little Kittens

Three little kittens
They lost their mittens,
And they began to cry,
Oh, Mother dear,
We sadly fear
Our mittens we have lost.
What! lost your mittens,
You naughty kittens!
Then you shall have no pie.
Mee-ow, mee-ow, mee-ow.
No, you shall have no pie.

The three little kittens
They found their mittens,
And they began to cry,
Oh, Mother dear,
See here, see here,
Our mittens we have found.
Put on your mittens,
You silly kittens,
And you shall have some pie.
Purr-r, purr-r, purr-r,
Oh, let us have some pie.

The three little kittens
Put on their mittens
And soon ate up the pie;
Oh, Mother dear,
We greatly fear
Our mittens we have soiled.
What! soiled your mittens,
You naughty kittens!
Then they began to sigh,
Mee-ow, mee-ow, mee-ow,
Then they began to sigh.

The three little kittens
They washed their mittens,
And hung them out to dry;
Oh, Mother dear,
Do you not hear,
Our mittens we have washed.
What! washed your mittens,
You good little kittens,
But I smell a rat close by.
Mee-ow, mee-ow, mee-ow,
We smell a rat close by.

The Potato with Big Ideas

Alf Prøysen

There was once a potato which lay waiting for someone to come and dig it up. The other potatoes were just quietly growing larger and larger, but this particular potato had ideas; he was stuck-up. And he was bored with waiting.

"Hi, everybody!" the stuck-up potato said. "I'm not going to wait any longer. I'll try to get out of this hole by myself. People must be longing to see what a beautiful potato I am; everything that is beautiful must see the light of day and enjoy the sunshine. Here I come! The most beautiful potato in all the world!"

You may know that all potatoes are tied to the mother potato by a thin thread (so that she can keep them in order, no doubt). Now that stuck-up potato began tugging at his thread, and the thread stretched and stretched till one fine day the stuck-up potato found himself lying on the ground above.

"Hurrah, hurrah! Here I am at last! Good morning, Mr. Weed! Good morning, Mrs. Worm! I am the world's most beautiful potato.

And if you, Mr. Sun, would like to shine on me for a moment, you can."

"With the greatest of pleasure," answered the sun, "but it won't be good for you, you know."

"Who cares? You just shine away and let me enjoy a nice hot sun-bath."

So the sun shone on the stuck-up potato and turned him blue, green, red, and purple all over. This made the potato more pleased with himself than ever:

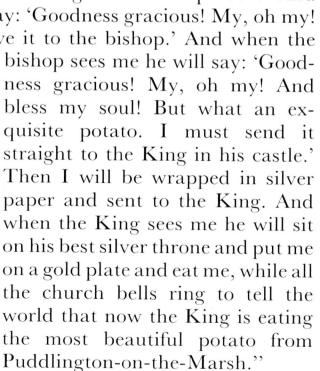

"When the boys come past and see me lying here they will say: 'My goodness! What a fine potato! We must take that home to Mother for dinner.' And one of them will put me carefully in his pocket. When his mother sees me she will say: 'Goodness gracious! What a wonderful potato; it's much too good for me. I will give it to the parson.' And when the parson sees me he will say: 'Goodness gracious! My, oh my! What a marvelous potato; I'll give it to the bishop.' And when the

bishop sees me he will say: 'Goodness gracious! My, oh my! And bless my soul! But what an exquisite potato. I must send it straight to the King in his castle.' Then I will be wrapped in silver paper and sent to the King. And when the King sees me he will sit on his best silver throne and put me on a gold plate and eat me, while all the church bells ring to tell the world that now the King is eating the most beautiful potato from Puddlington-on-the-Marsh."

But just as the potato was having this lovely dream, the farmer and his wife and their little boy came out into the field to start lifting potatoes.

They sang as they worked, and shouted to each other every time they found a really whopping big potato.

"Wait till they see *me*, then they'll have something to crow about!" thought the stuck-up potato.

Suddenly the little boy shouted: "Look at this funny-looking potato! It's blue and red and green all over!"

"Throw it in the pig bucket," said his father; "you can't eat that sort. It's been on top of the earth instead of underneath, where it should have been. But the pigs won't mind what color it is."

And so the stuck-up potato ended his days in the pig trough instead of on a gold plate in the King's castle, which all goes to show that even if you have big ideas it's sometimes wiser to be patient.

Monday's Child

Monday's child is fair of face,
Tuesday's child is full of grace,
Wednesday's child is full of woe,
Thursday's child has far to go,
Friday's child is loving and giving,
Saturday's child works hard for its living,
But the child that's born on the Sabbath day
Is fair and wise, and good and gay.

Tim Rabbit's Sneeze

Alison Uttley

One day it rained without stopping. The streams were swollen to little rivers, and new streams came running down the lanes, tearing up the stones, and sweeping the leaves before them. Pools formed in the hollows, and ponds filled every hole and dimple on the common. Little Tim Rabbit stood at the door of the small cottage watching the bouncing rain.

"Can I go out, Mother?" he asked.

"No, Tim," said Mrs. Rabbit, shaking her head. "No. You would get wet to your skin."

"I wish I had a mushroom umbrella," sighed Tim.

Five minutes later he asked again.

"Can I go fishing, Mother?"

"Certainly not," said Mrs. Rabbit. "Even the fish have gone into their houses to play."

"I wish I were a fish," sighed Tim.

He took a piece of chalk and made some squares on the kitchen floor. Then he played hopscotch, dancing and hopping in and out of the squares, with a stone balanced on his fur toe.

At last the rain stopped and the sun began to shine with a watery face. Tim looked out at the wet world. "Can I go out now, Mother?" he asked.

"Yes, Tim, but keep away from

the rain pools," said Mrs. Rabbit.

Tim fetched his fishing rod from the corner and ran outside. Every little pool and streamlet reflected the sunbeams. The common was all a-glitter. Raindrops shone like gold, and sparkled like fish scales.

"There must be lots of goldfish there," thought Tim.

He went across the wet grass, and sat by the edge of a small newly-made pond. It was rippled with little waves, and each wave was tipped with sunlight. At the bottom of the water Tim could see the daisies and buttercups growing. He dipped his hazel rod into the pond and waited for a fish to bite.

From the bough of an overhanging tree a bird looked down. It spread its feathers to dry them in the sun, and lifted a leg, and winked at Tim.

"Tim Rabbit! Tim Rabbit!" it called. "You'll never catch a fish that way."

"Hallo, Magpie," said Tim, looking into the leafy branches at the bright eye and the gleaming feathers of the wicked bird.

"The goldfish won't nibble at your bait, Tim. They like something special," said the Magpie.

"What do they like?" asked Tim.

"Throw away your fishing rod and dangle your feet in the water. They will nibble your toes," said the Magpie.

"I shouldn't like that," said Tim, quickly.

"They have no teeth, Tim. They'll only tickle you. When you feel a sweet tickle, grab the little goldfish from the water."

"Thank you, Magpie, I never knew that," said Tim, humbly, and he dangled his little furry toes in the water. For a long time he sat, and the

27

sun went in, and the gold waves became dark. A cloud passed over the sky. Tim's toes were very cold and he shivered, and then he sneezed.

"What are you doing there, sitting in the water, Tim Rabbit?" scolded the Hedgehog.

"Fishing for goldfish," said Tim.

"There ain't no fish, goldfish or silverfish, in that rainwater pool. Get you home at once, Tim Rabbit, and warm yourself by the fire, or you'll catch a cold."

Tim climbed out of the water, and he sneezed again. He felt very wet and rather miserable. He ran unsteadily, for his legs were stiff.

"Mercy me, Tim!" cried Mrs. Rabbit. "Where have you been? Your feet are soaking wet, and your nose is blue and your eyes are watering." She held up her paws in horror. She seized her little son and dried him with a warm towel and rubbed him with hay. Then she put him on a stool near the fire.

"A-tishoo! A-tishoo!" sneezed Tim.

"Deary me," cried Mrs. Rabbit. "You'll sneeze the roof off. The house isn't as strong as it was. The roof was never mended after that gale in March."

Tim sneezed again, and the roof of the little house shook.

"I must send that sneeze away or the house will fall down," cried Mrs. Rabbit in alarm.

She made Tim some hot blackcurrant tea, and he sipped it. She poured out a pan of hot water and sprinkled yellow mustard flowers in it. Little Tim sat with his feet in the nice water, and the steam curled around his head, but still he sneezed.

"A-tishoo! A-tishoo!"

There came a knock at the door and the Hare looked in.

"What is the matter, Mrs. Rabbit? I heard a very loud A-tishoo come from your house, and I saw the roof-thatch wobble. Is it safe?"

"Little Tim has caught a sneeze," said Mrs. Rabbit.

"Where did you find it, Tim?" asked the Hare.

"I found it out fishing," said Tim, and his voice was croaky and muffled in the steam.

"Put a fur bandage round your throat," said the Hare. He pulled some fur from his pocket. It was soft gray fur.

"Oh, thank you. Thank you," said Mrs. Rabbit. "What a kind Hare you are!"

"I've been young myself, and I know about wet feet," said the Hare. "My son, Sam, comes home after fishing and this is how I cure his colds."

Mrs. Rabbit made the delicate fur into a bandage. She wrapped it around little Tim's neck. It was very comfortable and warm, but the tiny hairs tickled Tim's nose, and he sneezed more than ever.

"A-tishoo! A-tishoo!" went Tim.

The house shook, and a bit of the ceiling fell down.

"Oh, dear me!" cried Mrs. Rabbit, wringing her paws. "I'm sure the house will tumble to bits if I can't stop Tim from sneezing."

She put him to bed, in the corner of the kitchen by the fire, but still he sneezed.

There came another knock at the door.

Tap-tap! Tap-tap! A squirrel peeped in.

"Whatever is the matter, Mrs. Rabbit? Such loud A-tishoos come from your house, my oak tree rustles. Is there anything wrong?"

"Oh, Miss Squirrel!" cried Mrs. Rabbit, wiping her eyes on her apron. "Tim has caught a sneeze. He can't get rid of it. I'm afraid it will blow the roof off. What shall I do?"

"Give him a dose of dandelion syrup, sweetened with honey," said the Squirrel. "I always take it when I have a cold."

She put her paw in her bag and brought out a root of dandelion and a honeycomb.

"Oh, thank you! Thank you, Miss Squirrel!" said Mrs. Rabbit. "What a kind Squirrel you are!"

She made the dandelion syrup, and gave Tim a spoonful. It was very soothing to his throat, but he sneezed again.

"A-tishoo! A-tishoo!" he went, and the picture of Snow White fell from the wall with a clatter.

"Oh, deary me," cried Mrs. Rabbit. "Our best picture broken. The house will never stand the strain of this."

She patted Tim and muffled him up, and put a log on the fire.

There came a tiny tap on the door. It was such a little tap it could hardly be heard, Tim was sneezing so loudly.

A Hen walked in, with little beak uplifted and wings fluttering anxiously.

"What is the matter, Mrs. Rabbit?" she clucked. "I was walking your way with my husband the

Cock for company and I heard the A-tishoos. Is anything wrong?"

"Oh, Mrs. Hen," sighed Mrs. Rabbit. "My Tim has caught a sneeze, and he cannot get rid of it. I'm afraid it will blow our house down. What shall I do?"

"Give him an egg well beaten, and mixed with a pinch of poppy dust," said the Hen. "I always take poppy dust for a cold."

She laid a brown egg on the floor, there and then.

"Oh, thank you! Thank you!" cried Mrs. Rabbit. She broke the egg into a bowl and beat it to a froth with a twig and dropped a pinch of poppy dust into it. Then she gave it

to Tim. "A-tishoo! A-tishoo!" he went, and the roof moved and shook.

He only sneezed the more.

There came a gentle push at the door and a Cow mooed softly outside.

"Whatever is the matter, Mrs. Rabbit?" she lowed. "The cattle are troubled by the loud A-tishoos coming from your cottage. Can I help you?"

"Oh, Mrs. Cow. Mrs. Mooley-Cow," cried Mrs. Rabbit. "My little Tim has caught a sneeze, and we cannot get rid of it. What shall I do?"

"Give him a mug of warm milk,"

said the Cow. She stood still by the door while Mrs. Rabbit milked her into a bowl.

"Oh, thank you! Thank you, Mrs. Cow," said the Rabbit. "What a kind Cow you are!"

She poured the warm frothy milk into Tim's own china mug, and held it out to Tim. He drank and he drank. He smiled happily, for he felt much better. Then suddenly he sneezed again.

"A-tishoo."

It was such a loud sneeze that everybody and everything seemed to listen.

Tap! Tap-tap! Tap-tap-tap! Who was that at the door? Mrs. Rabbit looked at Tim and Tim looked at Mrs. Rabbit.

"Who's there?" called Mrs. Rabbit.

Tap! Tap-tap! Tap-tap-tap!

The tip of a long red nose and white teeth came through the little door. It was the Fox himself.

"What is the matter, Mrs. Rabbit?" he asked, in his smooth oily voice. "I can get no peace for the loud A-tishoos that come from your house."

"Oh, Mr. Fox," stammered Mrs. Rabbit, and she trembled with fright. "My little Tim has caught a sneeze, and it won't go. I'm very sorry, Sir. I don't want to trouble you, Sir. I'm afraid it will blow my roof off, and we shall have no home. What shall I do, Sir?"

"Let me in, Mrs. Rabbit. I'm a first-class doctor. I can cure any rabbit of a cold. Open the door very wide, so that I can get in."

"Oh, no, Mr. Fox," said Mrs. Rabbit, and she looked at Tim. Tim shook his head.

"I want to feel his pulse, poor Tim Rabbit," said the Fox in a wheedling tone. "I will drive that sneeze away."

"Oh, no, Mr. Fox," said Mrs. Rabbit stoutly. "You might eat us, pulse and all. Oh, no, thank you. I would rather have the sneeze than the cure."

"Just as you like, Mrs. Rabbit. Keep your sneeze. I won't help you." The Fox snorted angrily and went away.

Little Tim Rabbit sat up in bed, and his eyes were bright. He was so frightened that he quite forgot to sneeze. Then away out of the chimney flew that sneeze, and the house stopped shaking and the roof settled comfortably again on the timbers.

Little Tim Rabbit cuddled close to his mother and in a minute he was fast asleep. In the morning the cold had quite gone.

As for the sneeze, it climbed to the top of the fir tree, and there it lives, A-tishooing when the wind blows hard. You can hear it if you listen on a cold winter's night when you are safe in bed.

Little Bo-peep

Little Bo-peep has lost her sheep,
And can't tell where to find them;
Leave them alone, and they'll come home,
Bringing their tails behind them.

Little Bo-peep fell fast asleep,
And dreamed she heard them bleating;
But when she awoke, she found it a joke,
For they were still a-fleeting.

Then up she took her little crook,
Determined for to find them;
She found them indeed, but it made her heart bleed
For they'd left their tails behind them.

It happened one day, as Bo-peep did stray
Into a meadow hard by,
There she espied their tails side by side,
All hung on a tree to dry.

She heaved a sigh, and wiped her eye,
And over the hillocks went rambling,
And tried what she could, as a shepherdess should,
To tack each again to its lambkin.

Town Mouse, Country Mouse

Aesop's Fables

There was once a little mouse who lived very happily in the country. He ate grains of wheat and grass seeds, nibbled turnips in the fields, and had a safe snug house in a hedgerow. On sunny days he would curl up on the bank near his nest and warm himself, and in the winter he would scamper in the fields with his friends.

He was delighted when he heard his cousin from the town was coming to visit him, and fetched some of the best food from his store cupboard so he could share it with him. When his cousin arrived, he proudly offered him some fine grains of dried wheat and some particularly good nuts he had put away in the autumn.

His cousin, the town mouse, however, was not impressed. "You call this good food?" he asked. "My dear fellow, you must come and stay with me in the city. I will then show you what fine living is all about. Come with me tomorrow."

So the two mice traveled up to town. From his cousin's mousehole, the country mouse watched with wonder as a grand dinner took place in the house. He stared in amazement at the cheese, the fresh white rolls, the fruit, and the wine served from glittering decanters.

"Now's our chance," said the town mouse, as the dining room emptied. The two mice came out of the hole, and scurried across the floor to where the crumbs lay scattered beneath the table. Never had the country mouse eaten such fine food. "My cousin was right," he

36

thought as he nibbled at a juicy grape. "This is the good life!"

All of a sudden a great fierce furry beast leaped into the room and pounced on the mice. "Run for it, little cousin!" shouted the town mouse, and together they reached the mousehole gasping for breath and shaking with fright. The cat settled down outside the hole, tail twitching, to wait for them.

"Don't worry. He will get bored soon, and go and amuse himself elsewhere. We can then go and finish our feast," said the town mouse.

"You can go out there again, if you like," said the country mouse. "I shall not. I am leaving tonight by the back door to return to my country home. I would rather gnaw a humble vegetable there than live here amidst these dangers."

So the country mouse lived happily in the country, the town mouse in the town. Each was content with the way of life he was used to, and had no desire to change.

I Love Little Pussy

I love little pussy,
Her coat is so warm,
And if I don't hurt her
She'll do me no harm.

So I'll not pull her tail,
Nor drive her away,
But pussy and I
Very gently will play.

She shall sit by my side,
And I'll give her some food;
And pussy will love me
Because I am good.

Milly-Molly-Mandy has a Surprise

Joyce Lankester Brisley

Once upon a time Milly-Molly-Mandy was helping Mother to fetch some jars of jam down from the little storeroom.

Father and Mother and Grandpa and Grandma and Uncle and Aunty and Milly-Molly-Mandy between them ate quite a lot of jam, so Mother (who made all the jam) had to keep the jars upstairs because the kitchen cupboard wouldn't hold them all.

The little storeroom was under the thatched roof, and it had a little square window very near to the floor, and the ceiling sloped away on each side so that Father or Mother or Grandpa or Grandma or Uncle or Aunty could stand upright only in the very middle of the room. (But Milly-Molly-Mandy could stand upright anywhere in it.)

When Mother and Milly-Molly-Mandy had found the jams they wanted (strawberry jam and blackberry jam and ginger jam), Mother said, "It is a pity I don't have somewhere else to keep my jam jars!"

And Milly-Molly-Mandy said, "Why, Mother, I think this is a very nice place for jam jars to live!"

And Mother said, "Do you?"

But a few days later Father and Mother went up to the little store-room together and took out all the jam jars and all the shelves that held the jam jars, and Father stood them down in the new shed he was making outside the back door, while Mother started cleaning out the little storeroom. Milly-Molly-Mandy helped by washing the little square window—"So that my jam

jars can see out!" Mother said.

The next day Milly-Molly-Mandy came upon Father in the barn, mixing paint in a bucket. It was a pretty color, just like a pale new primrose, and Milly-Molly-Mandy stirred it with a stick for a while, and then she asked what it was for. And Father said, "I'm going to paint the walls and ceiling of the little storeroom." And then he added, "Don't you think it will make the jam jars feel nice and cheerful?"

And Milly-Molly-Mandy said she was sure the jam jars would love it!

A little while afterward Mother sent Milly-Molly-Mandy to the village to buy a packet of green dye at Mr. Smale the Grocer's shop. And then Mother dyed some old casement curtains a bright green for the little storeroom window. "Because," said Mother, "the window looks so bare from outside."

And Mother decided she might as well dye the coverlet on Milly-Molly-Mandy's little cot-bed (which stood in one corner of Father and Mother's room), as the pattern had washed nearly white. So Milly-Molly-Mandy had a nice new bedspread, instead of a faded old one.

The next Saturday, when Grandpa came home from market, he brought with him a little chest of drawers, which he said he had "picked up cheap." He thought it might come in useful for keeping things in, in the little storeroom.

And Mother said, yes, it would come in very useful indeed. So (as it was rather shabby) Uncle, who had been painting the door of the new shed with apple-green paint, painted the little chest of drawers green too, so that it was a very pretty little chest of drawers indeed. "Well," said Uncle, "that ought to make any jam jar taste sweet!"

Milly-Molly-Mandy began to think the little storeroom would be almost too good just for jam jars.

Then Aunty decided she and Uncle wanted a new mirror in their room, and she asked Mother if their little old one couldn't be stored up in the little storeroom. And when Mother said it could, Uncle said he might as well use up the last of the green paint, so that he could throw away the tin. So he painted the frame of the mirror green.

"Jam jars don't want to look at themselves," said Milly-Molly-Mandy. She thought the mirror was far too pretty for the little store-room.

"Oh well—a mirror helps to make the room lighter," said Mother.

Then Milly-Molly-Mandy came upon Grandma embroidering a pretty little wool bird on either end of a strip of coarse linen. It was a robin, with a brown back and a scarlet front. Milly-Molly-Mandy thought it *was* a pretty cloth: and she wanted to know what it was for.

And Grandma said, "I just thought it would look nice on the little chest of drawers in the little storeroom." And then she added, "It might amuse the jam jars!" And Milly-Molly-Mandy laughed, and begged Grandma to tell her what the pretty cloth really was for. But Grandma would only chuckle.

The next day, when Milly-Molly-Mandy came home from school, Mother said, "Milly-Molly-Mandy, we've got the little storeroom in order again. Now, would you please run up and fetch me a jar of jam?"

Milly-Molly-Mandy said, "Yes, Mother. What sort?"

And Father said, "Blackberry."

And Grandpa said, "Ginger."

And Grandma said, "Plum."

And Uncle said, "Strawberry."

And Aunty said, "Raspberry."

But Mother said, "Any sort you like, Milly-Molly-Mandy!"

Milly-Molly-Mandy thought something funny must be going to happen, for Father and Mother and Grandpa and Grandma and Uncle and Aunty all looked as if they had got a laugh down inside them. But she ran upstairs to the little storeroom.

And when she opened the door—she saw—

Her little cot-bed with the green coverlet on, just inside. And the little square window with the green curtains blowing in the wind. And a yellow pot of nasturtiums on the sill. And the little green chest of drawers with the robin cloth on it. And the little green mirror hanging on the primrose wall, with Milly-Molly-Mandy's own face reflected in it.

And then Milly-Molly-Mandy knew that the little storeroom was to be her very own little bedroom, and she said "O-h-h-h!" in a very hushed voice, as she looked all around her room.

Then suddenly she tore downstairs back into the kitchen, and just hugged Father and Mother and Grandpa and Grandma and Uncle and Aunty; and they all said she was their favorite jam jar and pretended to eat her up!

And Milly-Molly-Mandy didn't know how to wait till bedtime, because she was so eager to go to sleep in the little room that was her Very Own!

42

Lavender's Blue

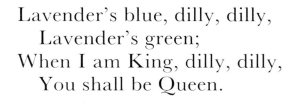

Lavender's blue, dilly, dilly,
  Lavender's green;
When I am King, dilly, dilly,
  You shall be Queen.

Call up your men, dilly, dilly,
  Set them to work,
Some to the plow, dilly, dilly,
  Some to the cart.

Some to make hay, dilly, dilly,
  Some to thresh corn,
Whilst you and I, dilly, dilly,
  Keep ourselves warm.

The Tiger Who Liked Baths

Donald Bisset

Once upon a time there was a tiger whose name was Bert. He had big, white, sharp teeth and when he growled it made a noise like thunder.

But Bert was a very nice tiger, always kind and gentle, except when someone else wanted to have a bath.

He loved having a bath and lay in the water all day until Mr. and Mrs. Smith and their baby daughter, who lived with him, were very cross. Because every time they wanted to have a bath Bert growled and showed his teeth.

"Come on, Bert! Do come out and have your supper," said Mrs. Smith, holding out a big plate of bones.

"No, thank you," said Bert, and growled.

Poor Mrs. Smith nearly cried. "It's time to bath the baby," she said, "and there's Bert still in the bath. Whatever shall I do?"

"I know what we'll do," said Mr. Smith, and he went and bought twenty bottles of black ink and, when Bert wasn't looking, he poured them into his bath. It made the water all black so that Bert got all black too.

A few hours later, Bert decided it was supper time so he got out of the bath.

"Oh, look at that big black pussy-cat," said Mr. Smith.

"Oh yes, what a beautiful pussy-cat!" said Mrs. Smith.

"Pussy-cat?" said Bert. "I'm not a pussy-cat. I'm a tiger."

"Tigers have stripes," said Mr. Smith. "They are not black all over like you."

"Oh dear!" said Bert. "Perhaps I am a pussy-cat after all."

"And pussy-cats," said Mr. Smith, "don't like having baths. You know that!"

"That's true!" said Bert.

After supper Bert went into the garden. And Prince, the dog next door, who liked chasing pussy-cats, saw Bert, and said, "There's a pussy-cat! I'll chase him!"

He felt a bit nervous because Bert looked the biggest pussy-cat he had ever seen. Still, pussy-cats had always run away before when he barked at them so he ran up to Bert, barking and showing his teeth.

Bert turned his head lazily and growled just once, like this: GRRRRR-RRRRRRRR!

Prince had never been so frightened in his life, and he jumped over the fence and ran home.

A little later, when Mr. Smith came into the garden, Bert asked him, "Am I really a pussy-cat? Don't you think I'm too big?"

"Well, you're not *really* a pussy-cat," said Mr. Smith. "You're a tiger. A special kind of tiger, who never likes staying in the bath for more than half an hour. And that's the very best kind of tiger."

Bert *was* pleased. "That kind!" he said to himself. "The very best kind!" And he purred and then licked all the black off till he was a lovely yellow tiger again with black stripes.

Then he went into the house and said to Mr. Smith, "I think I'll just go and have a bath." And he turned the water on and had a lovely bath. But he stayed in the water only for half an hour, and Mrs. Smith said he was a very good tiger and gave him a big bucket of ice cream.

Bert put his head in the bucket and licked. "Yum! Yum! Yum!" he said. "I do like ice cream."

Five Little Monkeys

Five little monkeys walked
along the shore;

Four little monkeys climbed
up a tree;

Three little monkeys found
a pot of glue;

Two little monkeys found
a currant bun;

One little monkey cried all
afternoon;

One went a-sailing,
Then there were four.

One tumbled down,
Then there were three.

One got stuck in it,
Then there were two.

One ran away with it,
Then there was one.

So they put him in an airplane
And sent him to the moon.

The Little Girl Who Got Out of Bed on the Wrong Side

Ruth Ainsworth

There was once a little girl who got out of bed on the wrong side. Oh, how cross she was! Cross as two sticks! She made a terrible fuss getting dressed. She complained that her sweater was tickly. She put her feet into the wrong shoes.

When she came down to breakfast, things were even worse. Her porridge was too hot. The milk was too cold. And her banana had black specks in it.

"I won't eat my horrid breakfast," said the little girl.

The kitten hid under the sofa and the puppy went into the brush cupboard and closed his eyes and pretended he wasn't there. The little girl was rather sorry, because she liked playing with the kitten and the puppy.

Everyone in the house left her alone and hoped she would soon feel better.

During the morning, her mother was busy making the Christmas treats. When she had the mixture ready in her big mixing bowl, it looked delicious and smelled even more delicious. She asked the little girl if she would like to stir the batter and make a wish.

"You'd better wish to be a happy girl," said her mother.

The little girl took the tall wooden spoon and stirred around and around, and as she stirred she *did* wish to be a happy girl. The wish came true even before she had licked the spoon. The kitten came out from under the sofa, the puppy came out of the cupboard, and they had a lovely game all over the house.

When lunchtime came, the little girl ate all her food. Afterwards, she went upstairs for her nap and the kitten and the puppy had their naps, too. When she woke up, she was very careful to get out of her bed on the *right* side.

Little Miss Muffet

Little Miss Muffet
 sat on a tuffet,
Eating her curds and whey;
There came a big spider,
 who sat down beside her
And frightened Miss Muffet away.

The Stamping Elephant

Anita Hewett

Elephant stamped about in the jungle, thumping down his great gray feet on the grass and the flowers and the small soft animals.

He squashed the tiny shiny creatures and trod on the tails of the creeping creatures. He beat down the corn seedlings, crushed the lilacs, and stamped on the morning glory flowers.

"We must stop all this stamping," said Goat, Snake, and Mouse.

Goat said, "Yes, we must stop it. But *you* can't do anything, Mouse."

And Snake said, "Of course she can't. Oh no, *you* can't do anything, Mouse."

Mouse said nothing. She sat on the grass and listened while Goat told his plan.

"Scare him, that's what I'll do," said Goat. "Oh good good good, I'll scare old Elephant, frighten him out of his wits I will."

He found an empty turtle shell and hung it up on a low branch. Then he beat on the shell with his horns.

"This is my elephant-scaring drum. I shall beat it, clatter clatter," he said. "Elephant will run away. Oh, good good good."

Stamp, stamp, stamp. Along came Elephant.

Goat tossed his head and ran at the shell, clatter, clatter, beating it with his horns.

"Oh, what a clatter I'm mak-

51

ing," he bleated. "Oh, what a terrible, elephant-scaring, horrible clatter."

Elephant said, "*What* a nasty little noise!"

He took the shell in his long trunk, lifted it high up into the air, and banged it down on Goat's hairy head. Then he went on his way, stamping.

Mouse said nothing. But she thought, "Poor old Goat looks sad, standing there with a shell on his head." Then she sat on the grass and listened while Snake told his plan.

"I shall make myself into a rope," said Snake. "Yes yes yes, that's what I'll do." He looped his body around a tree trunk. "Now I'm an elephant-catching rope. Yes yes yes, that's what I am. I shall hold old Elephant tight by the leg, and I shan't let him go. No, I shan't let him go, till he promises not to stamp any more."

Stamp, stamp, stamp. Along came Elephant.

Snake hid in the long grass. Elephant stopped beside a tree, propped up his two white tusks on a branch, and settled himself for a nice little sleep.

Snake came sliding out of the grass. He looped his long body around the tree trunk and around old Elephant's leg as well. His teeth met his tail at the end of the loop, and he bit on his tail tip, holding fast.

"I have looped old Elephant's leg to the tree trunk. Now I must hold on tight," he thought.

Elephant woke, and tried to move. But with only three legs he was helpless.

"Why are you holding my leg?" he shouted.

Snake kept quiet. He could not speak. If he opened his mouth the loop would break.

Elephant put his trunk to the ground and filled it with tickling yellow dust. Then he snorted, and blew the dust at Snake.

Snake wriggled. He wanted to sneeze.

Elephant put his trunk to the ground and sniffed up more of the tickling dust. "Poof!" he said, and he blew it at Snake.

Snake held his breath and wriggled and squirmed, trying his hardest not to sneeze. But the dust was too tickly. "Ah ah ah!" He closed his eyes and opened his mouth. "Ah ah tishoo!" The loop was broken.

Elephant said, "*What* a nasty little cold!"

And he went on his way, stamping.

Mouse said nothing. But she thought, "Snake looks sad, lying there sneezing his head off." Then she sat on the grass and made her own plan.

Stamp, stamp, stamp. Along came Elephant. Mouse peeped out of her hole and watched him. He lay on his side, stretched out his legs, and settled himself for a nice long sleep.

Mouse breathed deeply, and stiffened her whiskers. She waited till Elephant closed his eyes. Then she crept through the grass like a little gray shadow, her bright

brown eyes watching Elephant's trunk. She made her way slowly around his great feet, and tiptoed past his shining tusks. She trotted along by his leathery trunk until she was close to its tender pink tip. Then suddenly, skip! she darted backward, and sat in the end of Elephant's trunk.

Elephant opened his eyes, and said: "Can't I have *any* peace in this jungle? First it's a silly clattering goat, then it's a sillier sneezing snake, and now it's a mouse, the smallest of all, and quite the silliest. That's what *I* think."

He looked down his long gray trunk and said, "Oh yes, I know you are there, little mouse, because I can see your nose and whiskers. Out you get! Do you hear, little mouse?"

"Eek," said Mouse, "I won't get out, unless you promise not to stamp."

"Then I'll shake you out," Elephant shouted, and he swung his trunk from side to side.

"Thank you," squeaked Mouse. "I'm having a ride. It's almost like flying. Thank you, Elephant."

Elephant shouted, "I'll drown you out." He stamped to the river and waded in, dipping the end of his trunk in the water.

"Thank you," squeaked Mouse. "I'm having a swim. It's almost like diving. Thank you, Elephant."

Elephant stood on the bank, thinking. He could not pull down leaves for his dinner. He could not give himself a bath. He could not live, with a mouse in his trunk:

"Please, little mouse, get out of my trunk. Please," he said.

"Will you promise not to stamp?" asked Mouse.

"No," said Elephant.

"Then this is what I shall do," said Mouse, and she tickled his trunk with her tail.

"Now will you promise not to stamp?"

"No," said Elephant.

"Then this is what I shall do," said Mouse, and she nipped his trunk with her sharp little teeth.

"Yes," squealed Elephant. "Yes yes yes."

Mouse ran back to her hole, and waited.

Step, step, step. Along came Elephant, walking gently on great gray feet. He saw the tiny shiny creatures, and waited until they scuttled away. He saw the little creeping creatures, and stepped very carefully over their tails.

"Elephant doesn't stamp any more. *Someone* has stopped him," the creatures said. "Someone big and brave and clever."

Goat said: "I think Mouse did it."

And Snake said: "Oh yes, that is right. Mouse did it."

And not far away, at the foot of a tree, a small, contented, tired little mouse sat on the grass and smiled to herself.

Little Boy Blue

Little Boy Blue,
Come blow your horn.
The sheep's in the meadow,
The cow's in the corn.
Where is the boy
Who looks after the sheep?
He's under a haystack
Fast asleep.
Will you wake him?
No, not I,
For if I do,
He's sure to cry.

Teddy Robinson's Night Out

Joan G. Robinson

Teddy Robinson was a nice, big, comfortable, friendly, teddy bear. He had light brown fur and kind brown eyes, and he belonged to a little girl called Deborah. He was Deborah's favorite teddy bear, and Deborah was Teddy Robinson's favorite little girl, so they got along very well together, and wherever one of them went the other one usually went too.

One Saturday afternoon Teddy Robinson and Deborah looked out of the window and saw that the sun was shining and the almond tree in the garden was covered with pink blossom.

"That's nice," said Deborah. "We can play out there. We will make our house under the little pink tree, and you can get brown in the sun, Teddy Robinson."

So she took out a little tray with the dolls' tea-set on it, and a blanket to sit on, and the toy telephone in case anyone called, and she laid all the things out on the grass under the tree. Then she fetched a coloring book and some crayons for herself, and a book of nursery rhymes for Teddy Robinson.

Deborah lay on her tummy and colored the whole of an elephant and half a Noah's ark, and Teddy Robinson stared hard at a picture of

Humpty Dumpty and tried to remember the words. He couldn't really read, but he loved pretending to.

"Hump, hump, humpety-hump," he said to himself over and over again; and then, "Hump, hump, humpety-hump, Deborah's drawing an elephump."

"Oh, Teddy Robinson," said Deborah, "don't think so loud—I can't hear myself coloring." Then, seeing him still bending over his book, she said, "Poor boy, I expect you're tired. It's time for your rest now." And she laid him down flat on his back so that he could look up into the sky.

At that moment there was a loud *rat-tat* on the front door and a long ring on the doorbell. Deborah jumped up and ran indoors to see who it could be, and Teddy Robinson lay back and began to count the number of blossoms he could see in the almond tree. He couldn't count more than four because he only had two arms and two legs to count on, so he counted up to four a great many times over, and then he began counting backward, and the wrong way around, and any way around that he could think of, and sometimes he put words in between his counting, so that in the end it went something like this:

"*One, two, three, four,*
someone knocking at the door.
One, four, three, two,
open the door and how d'you do?
Four, two, three, one,
isn't it nice to lie in the sun?
One, two, four, three,
underneath the almond tree."

And he was very happy counting and singing to himself for quite a long time.

Then Teddy Robinson noticed that the sun was going down and there were long shadows in the garden. It looked as if it must be getting near bedtime.

Deborah will come and fetch me soon, he thought; and he watched the birds flying home to their nests in the trees above him.

A blackbird flew quite close to him and whistled and chirped, "Good night, teddy bear."

"Good night, bird," said Teddy Robinson and waved an arm at him.

Then a snail came crawling past.

"Are you sleeping out tonight? That will be nice for you," he said. "Good night, teddy bear."

"Good night, snail," said Teddy Robinson, and he watched it crawl slowly away into the long grass.

She will come and fetch me soon, he thought. It must be getting quite late.

But Deborah didn't come and fetch him. Do you know why? She was fast asleep in bed!

This is what had happened. When she ran to see who was knocking at the front door, Deborah found Uncle Michael standing on the doorstep. He had come in his new car, and he said there was just time to take her out for a ride if she came quickly, but she must hurry because he had to get into the town before dinner time. There was only just time for Mummy to get Deborah's coat on and wave goodbye before they were off. They came home ever so much later than they meant to because they had stopped for a snack, and then on the way home the new car suddenly stop-ped and it took Uncle Michael a long time to find out what was wrong.

By the time they reached home Deborah was half asleep, and Mummy had bundled her into bed before she had time to really wake up again and remember about Teddy Robinson still being in the garden.

He didn't know all this, of course, but he guessed something unusual must have happened to make Deborah forget about him.

Soon a little wind blew across the garden, and down fluttered some blossom from the almond tree. It fell right in the middle of Teddy Robinson's tummy.

"Thank you," he said, "I like pink flowers for a blanket."

So the almond tree shook its branches again, and more and more blossoms came tumbling down.

The garden tortoise came tramping slowly past.

"Hallo, teddy bear," he said. "Are you sleeping out? I hope you won't be cold. I felt a little breeze blowing up just now. I'm glad I've got my house with me."

"But I have a fur coat," said Teddy Robinson, "and pink blossom for a blanket."

"So you have," said the tortoise. "That's lucky. Well, good night," and he drew his head into his shell and went to sleep close by.

The next-door kitten came padding softly through the grass and rubbed against him gently.

"You *are* out late," she said.

"Yes, I think I'm sleeping out tonight," said Teddy Robinson.

"Are you?" said the kitten. "You'll love that. I did it once, I'm going to do it a lot oftener when I'm older. Perhaps I'll stay out tonight."

But just then a window opened in the house next door and a voice called, "Puss! Puss! Puss! Come and have your fish! fish! fish!" and the kitten scampered off as fast as she could go.

Teddy Robinson heard the window shut down and then everything was quiet again.

The sky grew darker and darker blue, and soon the stars came out. Teddy Robinson lay and stared at them without blinking, and they twinkled and shone and winked at him as if they were surprised to see a teddy bear lying in the garden.

And after a while they began to sing to him, a very soft and sweet and faraway little song, to the tune of *Rock-a-Bye Baby*, and it went something like this:

> *"Rock-a-bye Teddy, go to sleep soon.*
> *We will be watching, so will the moon.*
> *When you awake with dew on your paws*
> *Down will come Debbie and take you indoors."*

Teddy Robinson thought that was a lovely song, so when it was finished he sang one back to them. He sang it in a grunty voice because he was rather shy, and it went something like this:

"This is me
under the tree,
the bravest bear you ever did see.
All alone
so brave I've grown,
I'm camping out on my very own."

The stars nodded and winked and twinkled to show that they liked Teddy Robinson's song, and then they sang *Rock-a-bye Teddy* all over again, and he stared and stared at them until he fell asleep. Very early in the morning a blackbird whistled, then another blackbird answered, and then all the birds in the garden opened their beaks and twittered and cheeped and sang. And Teddy Robinson woke up.

One of the blackbirds hopped up with a worm in his beak.

"Good morning, teddy bear," he said. "Would you like a worm for your breakfast?"

"Oh, no, thank you," said Teddy Robinson. "I don't usually bother about breakfast. Do eat it yourself."

"Thank you, I will," said the blackbird, and he gobbled it up and hopped off to find some more.

Then the snail came slipping past.

"Good morning, teddy bear," he said. "Did you sleep well?"

"Oh, yes, thank you," said Teddy Robinson.

The next-door kitten came scampering up, purring.

"You lucky pur-r-son," she said as she rubbed against Teddy Robinson. "Your fur-r is damp but it was a pur-r-fect night for staying out. I didn't want to miss my fish supper last night, otherwise I'd have stayed with you. Pur-r-haps I

will another night. Did you enjoy
it?"

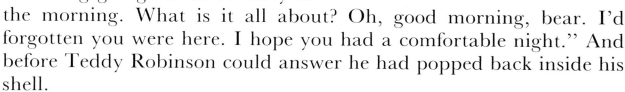

"Oh, yes," said Teddy Robinson. "You were quite right about
sleeping out. It was lovely."

The tortoise poked his head out
and blinked.

"Hello," he said. "There's a lot
of talking going on for so early in
the morning. What is it all about? Oh, good morning, bear. I'd
forgotten you were here. I hope you had a comfortable night." And
before Teddy Robinson could answer he had popped back inside his
shell.

Then a moment later Teddy Robinson heard a little shuffling noise
in the grass behind him, and there was Deborah out in the garden with
bare feet, and in her pajamas!

She picked him up and hugged him and kissed him and whispered to
him very quietly, and then she ran through the wet grass and in at the
kitchen door and up the stairs into her own room. A minute later she
and Teddy Robinson were snuggled down in her warm little bed.

"You poor, poor boy," she whispered as she stroked his damp fur. "I
never meant to leave you out all night. Oh, you poor, poor boy."

But Teddy Robinson whispered back, "I aren't a poor boy at all. I
was camping out, and it was lovely." And then he tried to tell her all
about the blackbird, and the snail, and the tortoise, and the kitten, and
the stars. But because it was really so very early in the morning, and

Deborah's bed was really so very
warm and cosy, they both got
drowsy; and before he had even got
to the part about the stars singing
their song to him, both Teddy
Robinson and Deborah were fast
asleep.

The Old Woman and her Pig

English Traditional

There was once an old woman who said, "What a fine morning, I think I will go to market today and buy a pig." So off she went to market and bought herself a handsome pig.

On her way home she took a short cut through some fields. She came to a stile, but whatever she said the pig just would not climb over. The old woman did not know what to do.

Then the old woman saw a dog so she said:
"Dog! Dog! Bite the pig!
The pig won't climb over the stile,
and I shan't get home tonight!"
But the dog would not bite the pig.
Then the old woman saw a stick, and she said:
"Stick! Stick! Beat the dog!
The dog won't bite the pig,
The pig won't climb over the stile,
and I shan't get home tonight!"
But the stick would not beat the dog.

The old woman found a fire, so she said:
"Fire! Fire! Burn the stick!
The stick won't beat the dog,
The dog won't bite the pig,
The pig won't climb over the stile,
and I shan't get home tonight!"
But the fire would not burn the stick.

The old woman was getting very cross, when she saw a bucket of water. So she said:

"Water! Water! Put out the fire!
The fire won't burn the stick,
The stick won't beat the dog,
The dog won't bite the pig,
The pig won't climb over the stile,
and I shan't get home tonight!"
But the water would not put out the fire.

The old woman went a little farther and she saw a bull standing in the field. So she said:

"Bull! Bull! Drink the water!
The water won't put out the fire,
The fire won't burn the stick,
The stick won't beat the dog,
The dog won't bite the pig,
The pig won't climb over the stile,
and I shan't get home tonight!"
But the bull would not drink the water.

The old woman went a little farther and met a butcher. So she said:

"Butcher! Butcher! Kill the bull!
The bull won't drink the water,
The water won't put out the fire,
The fire won't burn the stick,
The stick won't beat the dog,
The dog won't bite the pig,
The pig won't climb over the stile,
and I shan't get home tonight!"
But the butcher would not kill the bull.
Then the old woman saw a rope, and she said:
"Rope! Rope! Tie up the butcher!
The butcher won't kill the bull,
The bull won't drink the water,
The water won't put out the fire,
The fire won't burn the stick,
The stick won't beat the dog,
The dog won't bite the pig,
The pig won't climb over the stile,
and I shan't get home tonight!"
But the rope would not hold the butcher.

Then the old woman saw a rat, and she said:
"Rat! Rat! Gnaw the rope!
The rope won't hold the butcher,
The butcher won't kill the bull,
The bull won't drink the water,
The water won't put out the fire,
The fire won't burn the stick,
The stick won't beat the dog,
The dog won't bite the pig,
The pig won't climb over the stile,
and I shan't get home tonight!"
But the rat would not gnaw the rope.
The old woman then saw a cat, and she said:
"Cat! Cat! Catch the rat!
The rat won't gnaw the rope,
The rope won't hold the butcher,
The butcher won't kill the bull,
The bull won't drink the water,
The water won't put out the fire,
The fire won't burn the stick,
The stick won't beat the dog,
The dog won't bite the pig,
The pig won't climb over the stile,
and I shan't get home tonight!"

The cat said, "If you bring me a saucer of milk I will catch the rat for you."

The old woman jumped for joy and ran over to a cow in the next field, crying, "Cow! Cow! Will you give me some milk for the cat?" and the cow said, "If you bring me some hay from that haystack over there I will give you some milk."

So the old woman fetched some hay for the cow and the cow let the old woman milk her. She took the milk to the cat and the cat lapped it all up.

Then the cat began to chase the rat,
The rat began to gnaw the rope,
The rope began to hold the butcher,
The butcher began to kill the bull,
The bull began to drink the water,
The water began to put out the fire,
The fire began to burn the stick,
The stick began to beat the dog,
The dog began to bite the pig,
The pig leaped over the stile,
and the old woman got home that night!

Mr. Puffblow's Hat

Alf Prøysen

There was once a man called Mr. Puffblow who had an enormous hat. Mr. Puffblow was a very severe sort of man, and when he walked down the street he used to get very angry indeed if any of the children stared at his hat. And if they as much as stopped and looked at the house where he lived he would rush out and chase them off, because he thought they wanted to steal his apples.

Nobody dared go against Mr. Puffblow. "Ssh!" mothers would say to their children playing in the street. "You'd better be quiet—Mr. Puffblow is coming this way!"

Every day at precisely half past eleven Mr. Puffblow walked down the street to fetch his pint of milk from the dairy. So, until *that* was over, everybody stayed indoors.

One day the West Wind came tearing through the town, and I don't think there is anything like the West Wind for upsetting things in the autumn; the mischief it gets up to is nobody's business.

Now suddenly the West Wind caught sight of Mr. Puffblow walking down the street with his enormous hat on.

"Wheee!" said the West Wind. "That's just the hat for me!"

So, with a puff and a blow, it tipped Mr. Puffblow's hat off his head.

The hat bowled along the pavement. Mr. Puffblow ran after it. But just as he was about to catch it, the West Wind pounced and blew it further away. This game went on

for a long time until at last the West Wind carried the hat high up into the air, right over the rooftops of the town to the wood beyond.

"I'm tired of playing with you now," said the West Wind to the hat. "I'm going to drop you in this brook and leave you to sink or swim. Good luck!"

The hat turned two more somersaults in the air, then plopped into the brook and floated away like a little round ship.

It so happened that a tiny fieldmouse had been out in the wood that day gathering nuts, and he had fallen into the brook. He could swim all right, but the current was so strong he was almost drowned struggling against it.

When he saw the hat sailing past he caught hold of the brim with his paws and clambered up to the top of the crown.

"This would make a very good ship," thought the fieldmouse. "I wish some of the other mice could see me now." And he gave a loud squeak.

Sure enough, another fieldmouse heard him, and when he saw the fine-looking ship he called the other mice, and in the end there were

eight little fieldmice sailing along on the hat. The one who got on first was the captain, the second was his mate, and the rest were the crew.

You have no idea what fun those fieldmice had with Mr. Puffblow's hat that autumn! Every day they went for a sail, and when winter came and it got too cold, they dragged the hat onto dry land and used it for a house. All through the winter they sat inside it, snug and warm, telling each other mouse fairy tales and singing mouse carols at Christmas.

And when spring came they started sailing again.

Then one day there was a great noise and to-do in the wood. A whole crowd of children from the town were out for a picnic. There was a man with them and they were all laughing and shouting and having a fine time together. The man carried the smallest one on his shoulders while the others were clinging to his coat tails. They picked flowers for him and showed him all the nicest things they could find in the wood on a spring day.

Suddenly they stopped by the brook. "Look over there!" cried one of the children. "Look at that big hat on the other bank!"

The mice had just dragged the hat out of the brook because they

were going home to supper. When the man saw the hat he laughed and laughed. Because, you see, he knew it.

Can you guess who he was? Mr. Puffblow! But a very much nicer Mr. Puffblow now, and do you know why? Well, when he used to wear that enormous hat on his head he was always afraid the children would laugh at him. But from the moment he lost the hat he became quite different; he was no longer afraid.

"There's your old hat, Mr. Puffblow!" shouted the children with glee. "Don't you want to wear it again?"

"Certainly not!" said Mr. Puffblow. "Come along now, children, let's pick anemones."

So they did.

And the fieldmice are using Mr. Puffblow's hat for a ship to this day.

The Itsy Bitsy Spider

The Itsy Bitsy spider,
   Climbed up the waterspout;
Down came the rain
   And washed the spider out.
Out came the sunshine
   And dried up all the rain;
And the Itsy Bitsy spider,
   Climbed up the spout again.

The Little Wooden Horse

Ursula Moray Williams

One day Uncle Peder made a little wooden horse. This was not at all an extraordinary thing, for Uncle Peder made toys every day of his life, but oh, this was such a brave little horse, so gay and splendid on his four green wheels, so proud and dashing with his red saddle and blue stripes! Uncle Peder had never made so fine a little horse before.

"I shall ask five dollars for this little wooden horse!" he cried.

What was his surprise when he saw large tears trickling down the newly painted face of the little wooden horse.

"Don't do that!" said Uncle Peder. "Your paint will run. And what is there to cry about? Do you want more spots on your sides? Do you wish for bigger wheels? Do you creak? Are you stiff? Aren't your stripes broad enough? Upon my word I see nothing to cry about! I shall certainly sell you for five dollars!"

But the tears still ran down the newly painted cheeks of the little wooden horse, till at last Uncle Peder lost patience. He picked him up and threw him on the pile of wooden toys he meant to sell in the morning. The little wooden horse said nothing at all but went on crying. When night came and the toys slept in the sack under Uncle Peder's chair the tears were still running down the cheeks of the little wooden horse.

In the morning Uncle Peder picked up the sack and set out to sell his toys.

At every village he came to the children ran out to meet him, cry-

ing, "Here's Uncle Peder! Here's Uncle Peder come to sell his wooden toys!"

Then out of the cottages came the mothers and the fathers, the grandpas and the grandmas, the uncles and the aunts, the elder cousins and the godparents, to see what Uncle Peder had to sell.

The children who had birthdays were very fortunate: they had the best toys given to them, and could choose what they would like to have. The children who had been good in school were lucky too. Their godparents bought them wooden pencil boxes and rulers and paper cutters, like grown-up people. The little ones had puppets, dolls, marionettes, and tops. Uncle Peder had made them all, painting the dolls in red and yellow, the tops in blue, scarlet, and green. When the children had finished choosing, their mothers, fathers, grandpas, grandmas, uncles, aunts, elder cousins, and godparents sent them home, saying, "Now let's hear no more of you for another year!" Then they stayed behind to gossip with old Peder, who brought them news from other villages he had passed by on his way.

Nobody bought the little wooden horse, for nobody had five dollars to spend. The fathers and the mothers, the grandpas and the grandmas, the uncles and the aunts, the elder cousins and the god-parents, all shook their heads, saying, "Five dollars! Well, that's too much! Won't you take any less, Uncle Peder?"

But Uncle Peder would not take a penny less.

"You see, I have never made such a fine little horse before," he said.

All the while the tears ran down the nose of the little wooden horse, who looked very sad indeed, so that when Uncle Peder was alone once more he asked him, "Tell me, my little wooden horse, what is there to

cry about? Have I driven the nails crookedly into your legs? Don't you like your nice green wheels and your bright blue stripes? What is there to cry about, I'd like to know?"

At last the little wooden horse made a great effort and sobbed out, "Oh, master, I don't want to leave you! I'm a quiet little horse, I don't want to be sold. I want to stay with you for ever and ever. I shouldn't cost much to keep, master. Just a little bit of paint now and then; perhaps a little oil in my wheels once a year. I'll serve you faithfully, master, if only you won't sell me for five dollars. I'm a quiet little horse, I am, and the thought of going out into the wide world breaks my heart. Let me stay with you here, master—oh, do!"

Uncle Peder scratched his head as he looked in surprise at his little wooden horse.

"Well," he said, "that's a funny thing to cry about! Most of my toys want to go out into the wide world. Still, as nobody wants to give five dollars for you, and you have such a sad expression, you can stop with me for the present, and maybe I won't get rid of you after all."

When Uncle Peder said this the little wooden horse stopped crying at once, and galloped three times around in a circle.

"Why, you're a gay fellow after all!" said Uncle Peder, as the little wooden horse kicked his legs in the air, so that the four green wheels spun around and around.

"Who would have thought it," said Uncle Peder.

Wee Willie Winkie

Wee Willie Winkie
   Runs through the town,
Upstairs and downstairs
   In his nightgown.
Rapping at the window,
   Crying through the lock,
Are all the children in their beds,
   It's past eight o'clock?